See You Later, Jeffrey

See You Later Jeffrey

FRAN CAFFEY SANDIN

Tyndale House Publishers, Inc.
Wheaton, Illinois

The poem "The Weaver" is available in tract form
from the Faith, Prayer, and Tract League, Grand
Rapids, Michigan 49504. Used by permission.

"Heaven Is a Wonderful Place"—words and music
by O. A. Lambert, © 1958, © renewed 1986 by
Sacred Songs (a Div. of Word, Inc.). All rights
reserved. International copyright secured. Used by
permission.

A few names have been changed to protect the
privacy of the individuals involved.

Unless otherwise indicated, the Scriptures quoted
are from the New American Standard Version of *The
Holy Bible,* © 1960, 1962, 1963, 1968, 1971, 1972,
1973, 1975, 1977 by The Lockman Foundation, La
Habra, California.

First printing, November 1988
Library of Congress Catalog Card Number 88-72038
ISBN 0-8423-5872-2
© 1988 by Fran Caffey Sandin
All rights reserved
Printed in the United States of America

To my husband, Jim,
who lovingly encouraged me
in sharing our son's story

CONTENTS

ACKNOWLEDGMENTS

I'm blessed with a host of friends and relatives. Dear ones, your love and prayers gave me strength through the years to persevere.

I'm thankful for those who challenged me to continue writing: Dr. Bob E. Hamilton, Dr. A. Duane Litfin, Dr. Haddon W. Robinson, Nancy Bahm, Ed Wichern, Cherry Brown, and Linda Gilberto.

I'm also thankful for my efficient typists: Jill Baker, Mildred Campbell, Linda Hare, and Sandy Slack.

Two close friends and fellow writers who aided me in completing the manuscript are Thelma R. Hollingsworth and Linda R. McGinn.

I'm especially grateful to Tyndale House Editor-at-Large Virginia Muir, for her gracious encouragement and support.

I deeply appreciate each one of you. Thank you for caring, for sharing your time and talents, for weeping, and now rejoicing with me.

Isn't God wonderful?

O magnify the LORD with me, and let us exalt His name together. Psalm 34:3

He hath made everything beautiful in its time. Ecclesiastes 3:11

INTRODUCTION

In the days before the twentieth century, death usually occurred in the home. Now the dreadful enemy most often intrudes upon the medical center's sterile environment. As a young nurse in the hospital, I had occasion to stand alongside families as they faced the sorrow and loss of a loved one. Frightened, lonely, and away from familiar surroundings, the family members I came in contact with seemed to long for a caring touch.

They came with high expectations. With today's sophisticated technology, they knew that children and young adults rarely die. However, even the most elaborate hospital has no magical cure for the mortality of man. Death is something each of us must eventually face.

This fact became a shocking reality when one day I stood at the hospital bedside, not as a nurse, but as a mother. For the first time, I understood more completely what the grieving families had experienced. I, too, wrestled with the gripping fear of death.

It is not so much what we see and feel with our senses that disturbs us, but the mystery that lies beyond. There are questions to ponder, fears to address, and internal frustrations to resolve. Often it is impossible to verbalize our concerns to others.

That's why I'm sharing my story. Some of the questions and answers I've discovered may be helpful to you or someone you love. If just one person sees life from a new vantage point, then my effort will be worthwhile.

What a wonderful God we have—he is the Father of our Lord Jesus Christ, the source of every mercy, and the one who so wonderfully comforts and strengthens us in our hardships and trials. And why does he do this? So that when others are troubled, needing our sympathy and encouragement, we can pass on to them this same help and comfort God has given us. 2 Corinthians 1:3-4, TLB

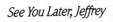
See You Later, Jeffrey

O N E
Here's Jeffrey

Behold, children are a gift of the LORD. Psalm 127:3

✻ Each Thursday I looked forward to a few hours to run errands and buy groceries while Steve, five, Angie, three, and Jeffrey, seventeen months, stayed at the church nursery for "Mother's Day Out."

Jeffrey was adorable. After dropping the children off, I had to turn and look one more time as he pressed his chubby hand against the church nursery window, waving good-bye. He was vivacious, smiling, chuckling. On that particular day, I took a few minutes to soak up the joy radiating from Jeffrey's countenance. I waved as I walked backward a few steps on the sidewalk. When I got in the car to drive away, the view of him gladdened my heart. Sometimes I was in a hurry to leave because of all I wanted to accomplish within the time limit; but that day, watching Jeffrey through the window seemed the most important item of all.

A few days later, as we were riding in the car, Steve was in the front seat with me, and Jeffrey and Angie were in the back. Jeffrey was strapped into his car seat. He enjoyed riding anywhere and was always ready to "go." As we rode along, he gazed intently out the window. When we stopped for a red light, I turned to look at him; he broke into a big grin. My Mother's Memory Camera clicked once again.

Ice cream cones were favorite treats for the children. Jeffrey had his own idea about how to eat one. He turned it upside down and ate the cone first, then tried to recover what remained of the ice cream! A messy technique . . . but *mmm-mmm* good.

Jeffrey never wanted to be last or left out of anything. When Jim came home from the office, Jeffrey often ran to the door saying, "Me, me, me," because he wanted to be greeted first.

He loved to sit in his dad's lap along with Steve and Angie. Intrigued with all the goodies in Jim's shirt pocket, he'd carefully remove ballpoint pens and papers one by one. After the evening meal and before bedtime, we played games as a family. Usually we were all on the floor playing Ring around the Rosey or London Bridge.

Jeffrey was always in the middle. Sometimes I think we could have charged admission for a three-ring show. Steve especially liked performing antics to entertain his little brother. Jeffrey had such an infectious chuckle that soon he'd start us all laughing. It was fun.

Angie and Steve shared a room with their little brother at different times. Angie and Jeffrey were roommates while Jeffrey was still in a crib. When Jeffrey graduated from the crib to a youth bed, he moved in with Steve. Keeping him in the youth bed was fine except at nap time. When he discovered the freedom of having no side rails, he just had to jump out of bed at least once before settling down to rest.

Not only did Jeffrey have a family who loved him, but he had extended family admirers. Grandparents, aunts, uncles, cousins—Jim and I have close family ties. Jim's mom had moved to Greenville to be near us. She was very sweet to come to our house and keep the children occasionally so Jim and I could have some time to ourselves. Grandma Sandin often sat in the big rocking chair in the family room with all three children, rocking and singing, "Jesus loves me, this I know—for the Bible tells me so. . . ."

Each of our children was special. Reflecting upon the day of Jeffrey's birth, I recall the joy that Jim and I felt as we "inspected" our son, cuddled him, and listened to his first cooing newborn sounds. It seems only yesterday that Jim entered the hospital room just as I had finished nursing Jeffrey and the three of us were alone.

I remember we looked into our son's face and beheld his expression of complete contentment. As I wrapped Jeffrey snugly in a warm blanket and held him closely, Jim sat on the bed beside me and, grasping my hand, led us in a prayer of dedication. "Dear heavenly Father, we thank You for the blessing of this son You have given us. We thank You for the gift of life and for allowing us the privilege of having Jeffrey. We realize the great responsibility we have as parents, and we pray that You will guide us as we seek to train our son in a way that will be pleasing to You. For it is in the name of Jesus that we pray, amen."

When our first two children were born, I was excited beyond measure. I expressed some of my exuberance in poetry—a poem for Steve and a poem for Angie. When Jeffrey was born, I didn't write a poem—there just wasn't one in my mind. Then a thought came to me while I was still in the hospital: *You wrote poems for Steve and Angie, but you will write a book about Jeffrey.* How absurd, I remember thinking! I was going home to take care of three preschoolers, and that was enough to keep me busy for a few years. So I forgot all about it.

Everything seemed perfect for us. Jim enjoyed his practice of urology, which filled a need in the community. I loved being a homemaker. Even though I experienced frustrating days, I felt fortunate to be at home with our children. We had met some wonderful friends, and most of our family was within a day's drive. I was counting my blessings, delighting in my attentive husband and healthy children, and looking toward a bright future. Then, suddenly, my life was changed.

T W O
One Empty Chair

And now, Lord, for what do I wait? My hope is in Thee.
Psalm 39:7

❋ On Sunday morning, April 28, 1974, Jeffrey cried, "Mama." I sprang from my bed and we met at his bedroom door. His arms were outstretched to me and I lifted him. Because his cheek felt warm against mine, I checked and found his temperature elevated to 102 degrees, so I gave him Tempra and juice.

Although Jeffrey was mentally alert, his body relaxed against mine as if he wanted to rest, so I rocked him in the chair near his bed. I wondered what caused Jeffrey's fever. He had seemed perfectly well the night before. A virus was "going around," and the children plagued with it had fever, but no other symptoms. Jeffrey must have been exposed to a sick child.

Although Jim and I were concerned, we felt this would be one of those short-lived childhood illnesses that come and go with the exact cause unknown. Liquids, rest, and medication seemed the reasonable treatment at the time. I stayed at home with Jeffrey while Jim took Steve and Angie to church.

Jeffrey slept while I proceeded with household chores, listened to a radio ministry entitled, "It Costs to Care," and began preparing lunch. There was a heaviness in my spirit that could not be explained. The physical symptoms Jeffrey had did not merit such a degree of concern, but I felt it anyway. I tried to ignore that feeling, thinking that as a nurse I often jumped to the most serious conclusion.

As we gathered around the table for Sunday lunch, Steve and Angie were asking questions. "Is Jeffrey sick? Can he eat with us?" they wanted to know. I explained that he drank some juice earlier and now he needed rest.

We said a special prayer for him. The four of us held hands and Jim prayed, "Dear heavenly Father, thank You for our home and for this food You have provided. Thank You for loving us. Please help Jeffrey to get well soon. In Jesus' name, amen."

After the prayer I looked at the empty high chair. I missed Jeffrey's smile. I even missed cleaning up the mess around the chair after lunch. I did not know that he would be absent from our mealtimes forever.

When Steve and Angie took a nap, so did I. Jeffrey seemed to be resting well so the house was very quiet.

About 4:00 P.M. Jim and I checked Jeffrey as I attempted to give him more liquids. He was pale, listless, and did not want to drink. Whatever the cause of his distress, his resistance was not working adequately, and he was not getting better. We called our pediatrician, who met us at the hospital emergency room. Our normally bubbly, responsive, active toddler was not talking. He was glassy-eyed and lethargic. I was scared.

As I carried his limp body into the emergency room, I cried out to God in my heart, *O, God, please help us! Jeffrey needs You.* Although I maintained outward composure, inwardly I was weak and quivering. I had difficulty recalling the information needed to fill out the admission form, but God was whispering an assuring message for the hours and days ahead. *Get ready. It will be dark, but I will be with you.* I did not understand.

While we waited in the doctor's lounge for the pediatrician's report, Jim was called out to care for a patient brought to the emergency room with a urological problem. When he finally returned, his expression was somber. Joining me on the sofa, he put his arm around me and confided, "The spinal fluid drawn from our son was cloudy. It looks like bacterial meningitis." He paused while I leaned against his shoulder, crying in disbelief.

He continued, "It appears we have an early start in treatment; with the intravenous fluids and antibiotics, Jeffrey should pull through. He'll be spending the night in the Intensive Care Unit so I suggest you run home and get what you need to stay here. I'll go home later to watch Steve and Angie to make sure they're not getting any symptoms." The exact type of meningitis was not yet known and some types are contagious. I could hardly take all of this in.

At home, while grabbing items for the overnight case, I remembered the church prayer group and how we had prayed on many occasions for illness to be relieved, and it was.

With trembling hands, I picked up the phone and dialed the number of a close friend. "Rosemary, we took Jeffrey to the hospital and he's very sick. Please pray."

With confidence in her voice, she said, "Don't worry, honey. We'll be praying for little Jeffrey. Everything will be OK." I hung up the receiver, encouraged to know that our church family would be praying for us. I felt the love of friends as a soothing balm.

After I returned to the hospital, knowing that Grandma Sandin and Jim would be at home with Steve and Angie for the night, I called another friend, Linda, to tell her about Jeffrey.

Linda and I had known each other for many years. We had been nursing students at Texas Woman's University together, and after graduation we kept in touch. Jim and Harold, Linda's husband, were friends, too. Subsequently, much to our surprise and delight, our families established permanent residences in the same community. Linda's friendship was comforting, especially now.

"Fran, you know meningitis is very serious," she reminded me. Yes, I did know, but I didn't want to think about it. At the close of our conversation, she said meaningfully, "Let me know if you need me." I clung to those words as I stepped into the Intensive Care Unit to spend the night.

THREE
Transfer to Dallas

But I, O LORD, have cried out to Thee for help, and in the morning my prayer comes before Thee.
Psalm 88:13

✸ I stayed at Jeffrey's side during the night. Gradually his ashen color changed to pink, and I felt relieved to see his cheeks were rosy again. But his lethargy was replaced by unpredictable motion of his arms and legs. That worried me because of the necessity of keeping his arm still. I watched the needle in his arm to make sure there was a proper flow of fluids into his vein. These intravenous fluids with antibiotics added were vital to his recovery.

He rested only intermittently, often tossing and turning from side to side, mumbling, "Mama, wanna go outside." I talked to him, whispered loving things, and kissed him, but fear was ever present within me.

When he was quiet, I read a few passages from the Bible. My thoughts drifted back to the days when, working on the pediatric unit at the University Hospital in Little Rock, Arkansas, I took care of patients with meningitis. I remembered that some began improvement after the first day or two and then slowly recovered—some completely; some with complications.

A few did not get well. Microscopic organisms—so tiny and yet so deadly! The battle raged within our son's body. Would the antibiotics overcome the bacteria and their potentially harmful effects?

Early Monday morning I began to notice twitching movements in Jeffrey's extremities. I called the nurse. While she stood there beside his bed, he began having episodes of violent jerking. I was alarmed by this quick progression into severe seizures. The nurse quickly called the doctor, who gave her instructions over the phone and then came to the Intensive Care Unit himself. In need of moral support at that point, I found a telephone and called Jim at home. He soon joined me in the Intensive Care waiting room.

WAITING. . . . I wanted to be with Jeffrey, but I simply could not bear to watch him suffer. Again Jim and I were alone. The seriousness and uncertainty of the moment was uppermost in our minds as Jim broke the silence with, "Remember that 2 Timothy 1:7 says God has not given us a spirit of fear, but of love, power, and a sound mind."

Tearfully we confessed our fears to each other, but agreed that if Jeffrey did not survive, he would certainly be one of God's favorites in heaven. It was the first time we communicated our apprehensions in words. At that instant we felt very close to God and to each other. As we embraced, we shared strength to face the day.

Time and familiar routine were of no consequence as we waited for the pediatrician's report. I called my dear friend, Linda, to share the latest developments. Even though it was 7:45 A.M., she quickly took care of details at home and arrived within minutes.

Caring friends from church also came—Eddie, and Johanna and David, our Bible study class teachers. They joined us in the hospital chapel for prayer. Eddie and David each voiced our sentiments, committing Jeffrey, the doctors, and all the events of the day into God's hands.

While Jeffrey rested quietly in response to sedation, the decision was made to transfer him to the Children's Medical Center in Dallas. Jim rode in the ambulance with Jeffrey and the pediatrician. I wanted to be with them also, but I was too emotionally upset and felt my presence might be a hindrance in the event of further crises. Johanna offered to take me in her car.

After the ambulance departed, we followed along on the thirty-mile trip. As Johanna and I talked, I somehow felt removed from the reality of the situation. Was this experience really happening to me? My attention span for conversation was brief. I knew in my heart that Johanna was joining me in constant, silent prayer for Jeffrey's safe arrival in Dallas.

I was overwhelmed by faithful friends who left their routine and responsibilities to give their time, love, and support. It was as though I was surrounded by a clear, protective bubble. As we pulled up to the hospital, my friends were standing there with open, loving arms and hugs, compassionate, tear-stained eyes, and hope for the hours ahead. My only thoughts were for Jeffrey. The compelling force that sent friends at just the right time matched my desperate need for each one.

FOUR
Thirty-six Hours

Peace I leave with you, my peace I give unto you; not as the world giveth, give I unto you. Let not your heart be troubled, neither let it be afraid. John 14:27, KJV

✳ At Children's Medical Center in Dallas, attendants were on hand to meet the ambulance and to wheel Jeffrey quickly into the emergency room. By 9:30 Monday morning, the best medical minds were at work on our son. The pediatricians spent almost three hours working with him and assessing his condition.

As Johanna and I walked into the hallway, I was surprised and delighted to see Suzanne, one of my former roommates from nursing school. She was the supervisor on duty and had heard that Jeffrey was being transferred in. She told her coworkers, "I know the baby's mother." I knew she was working in Dallas, but had not realized she was at Children's. We had not seen each other since graduation. Her presence gave me confidence that Jeffrey's nursing care would be excellent.

Before leaving Greenville, we had called my parents, Pratha and Billie Caffey, in Mineola, Texas. As I spoke with Mom, she asked "Fran, what would you like us to do?"

I felt the need of their support so I blurted out, "Please come." Mom cancelled her plans for the day, and Dad left his auto repair shop in Hawkins. Being wise parents, they packed a little suitcase. Later that morning, they arrived in Dallas and lovingly joined us in the waiting room.

The atmosphere there was tense as we nervously chatted to pass the time. Johanna thoughtfully gave me some writing pens and notepads. Linda provided pocket change for making long-distance telephone calls. At every turn, someone was ready to take care of our needs. My family and friends were a living illustration of Philippians 4:19, which says, "My God shall supply all your needs according to His riches in glory in Christ Jesus." God uses people to do His work on earth.

Finally, our pediatrician came to say he was returning to his office in Greenville. We were so thankful for him. No one could have asked for a more caring, conscientious doctor. He had extended himself in every way and had worked for hours in the emergency room along with the hospital staff. Jim assured him of our gratefulness and said, "Win, lose, or draw, everything will turn out all right because Jeffrey is in God's hands." I gave him a hug, and Jim extended a warm handshake, but our pediatrician returned to Greenville with a heavy heart.

At last, Dr. Hill emerged from behind closed emergency room doors to give us the long-awaited report. He said that Jeffrey had been treated early in the course of the illness and our pediatrician had done everything possible, but Jeffrey's case was unusual. Complications had developed rapidly.

Pneumonia had begun. There was also some hemorrhaging. Dr. Hill stated very frankly, "It will be thirty-six hours before we know if Jeffrey will turn the corner. During this critical time period, we will take every possible measure to help him through." After our discussion with Dr. Hill, attendants transferred Jeffrey to a private room.

Whatever took place in the succeeding minutes and hours is lost to my remembrance. All I could think of was Jeffrey. I felt awkward as I stood at his bedside. I was a nurse, but this time the sick child was my son. I was his mother, and the oxygen tent isolated him from me. My greatest desire was to remove everything and everyone and just sit by the window in the warm sunlight, rocking him, comforting him against my breast. I wanted to kiss his forehead and say, "Mom's here, and everything is going to be fine."

Instead, all the tubes and equipment necessary to his survival separated us, and I felt utterly helpless. He was pale and motionless. Over and over I thought to myself, *That really isn't Jeffrey, is it? This is not really happening, is it?*

A small speck of blood had dried on his cheek. The nurse handed me a washcloth and asked, "Would you like to wash Jeffrey's face?"

I took the warm, moist cloth in my hands and moved closer to the bed. I should have wanted to wash his face. I was his mother. But at home when I washed Jeffrey's face he laughed and played, and it was fun for both of us. Now he did not seem like my son at all, and I wanted to recoil. Inwardly I cried out to be near him, to love him and minister to him; yet I was almost repulsed by what I saw. The nurse looked at me sadly and seemed to understand. Together, we washed his face.

Monday was a long day. Fortunately, private duty nurses were available, so Mother spent the night in Jeffrey's room with the nurse while I sought rest on a couch in the main lobby downstairs. Jim returned to Greenville to check on Grandma, Steve, and Angie. Others left for home, and Dad spent the night with relatives in Dallas.

I was able to sleep for several hours. I'd awaken long enough to catch the elevator upstairs, check to see that Jeffrey was all right, then hurry back to the couch for more rest. The time spent there was peaceful and refreshing. It helped me to remember that God was "on duty" because He never sleeps. I frequently thought of Psalm 121:3-4, which says, "He who keeps you will not slumber. Behold, He who keeps Israel will neither slumber nor sleep."

Tuesday was a better day! Jeffrey appeared to respond to treatment. His color was greatly improved. At times when I spoke to him he would move an arm or a leg. Best of all, the hemorrhaging had decreased. I stood at his bedside just thanking God for answered prayer.

My eyes were drawn like a magnet to the large picture window in Jeffrey's room. Bright sunshine streamed in, the grass along the walkway below was rich and healthy, and colorful flowers edging the path announced spring's arrival. I could almost hear God saying, "See, I haven't forgotten you." With a spirit of euphoria, I turned to Psalm 116 and read every verse aloud to Jeffrey. Worship is not necessarily confined to a certain time or building!

I remained in a spirit of praise and thanksgiving as the entourage of residents, interns, and attending staff entered the room on their morning rounds.

"How does Jeffrey look to you?" asked Dr. Hill.

"Marvelous!" I quickly replied.

Their guarded expressions indicated they did not share my enthusiasm. One or two looked at me as though I needed a visit to the psychiatric ward. But in my heart I so wanted Jeffrey to turn the corner for good that I could not allow their pessimism to dampen my spirits. The physical improvements were not actually as great as I interpreted them to be, but I clung to every shred of evidence pointing toward hope.

My anxiety about Jeffrey's condition was alleviated to some extent by the presence and conversation of family and friends. Mother and Dad were in and out, always available. My brother and his wife, Lanny and Janice, came to join us. Debbie, my sister in college, was in touch and joined us later. Aunts, uncles, cousins, and friends in the Dallas area were so very solicitous. I received a happy surprise when another friend and former roommate from nursing school, Carolyn, took time from her busy schedule to come, offering sincere condolences and assistance.

We received several long-distance telephone calls from friends who reminded us of their concern and prayers. Jim and I remained constantly aware that we were loved and that people really cared about Jeffrey. No act of kindness, however small it may have seemed to the one performing it, went unnoticed.

Johanna and Linda kept me supplied with note cards for my purse. I thought of these cards as a mini-survival kit because they helped me focus upon a Power greater than my own, and I needed all the help I could get. Each card had a message. First Peter 5:7 was printed on one: "Casting all your anxiety upon Him, because He cares for you." Another was Isaiah 41:10, "Do not fear, for I am with you . . . I will help you, surely I will uphold you with My righteous right hand."

Once in a quiet moment, praying alone, I tried to visualize Jeffrey completely healed. As I looked around and saw little children running in the hospital hallway or playing in the playroom, I could imagine Jeffrey on a rocking horse—laughing, bouncing, full of life and joy. I could see his twinkling blue eyes and could feel his soft, blond, curly hair as I thought of a day in the future when he would sit on my lap and I would tell him of the time he had been very close to death. Would I ever have that opportunity?

F I V E
Code Blue

I will never desert you, nor will I ever forsake you.
Hebrews 13:5

✳ It was Wednesday, the third morning of Jeffrey's illness. The thirty-six hours had ended with no determining change in his condition. I had just come into his hospital room after a few hours of rest in the downstairs lobby. When I entered, Mother awakened after spending the night napping in the lounge chair near Jeffrey's bed, and together we visited with the private duty nurse coming to work for the 7:00 A.M. shift.

As we chatted, I observed the rise and fall of Jeffrey's small chest. The rhythmical movement suddenly stopped.

"Quick! Get help! Jeffrey is not breathing!" I cried. My first impulse was to shove the nurse aside and begin mouth-to-mouth resuscitation. Instead, I retreated in fear. The nurse flashed a message to the emergency room—CODE BLUE. Immediately, doctors and nurses ran from the nurses' station down the hall to Jeffrey's room.

The one person whom Jeffrey needed most was the pediatric anesthesiologist. He quickly appeared. Promptly, he placed a tube in Jeffrey's windpipe and began pumping oxygen into his lungs.

One attendant rushed by pushing a rolling cart loaded with extra equipment. As she wheeled the cart into the room, Mother and I stepped aside. A gentleman observed our dazed expressions and placed two chairs along the hallway outside Jeffrey's room. There we sat. I felt like a useless statue decorating the hospital corridor.

The competent, composed quick action of the staff left no doubt that Jeffrey was receiving the best possible attention. Occasionally a doctor or nurse would leave the room, slip out of sight briefly, then return. My eyes were glued to them as I desperately searched each face for some ray of hope. I saw none. Every countenance was grim.

I silently prayed, *O, Lord, why can't I be the one in that bed instead of our precious boy? It would be easier to bear this illness myself than to stand by and watch him suffer.*

The huge lump in my throat finally gave way to trickling tears. Mother reached over and placed her hand on mine. Although I was hurting and felt confused, I remembered a Bible verse. "I will never, never fail you nor forsake you" (Heb. 13:5, TLB). We were not alone.

After Mother and I had waited quite a long time, I

glanced up to see Dr. Hill approach. He greeted us with a sympathetic expression, apparently sensitive to my emotional turmoil. He invited us into a vacant room nearby, and when we were quietly settled he explained, "The reason Jeffrey stopped breathing was because of brain damage, either due to the toxicity of the bacteria or possibly due to a blood clot."

He continued, "Jeffrey was resuscitated and will remain on a respirator for twenty-four hours. We will watch him closely in the Intensive Care Unit. If there is any sign of improvement, however slight, we will notify you. If there is no indication of positive progress from this point, the chances that Jeffrey will live are very slim."

With tears in his eyes, he whispered, "I'm so sorry." His message pierced my heart like a knife. He hugged me briefly and asked if I had any questions. I was speechless and just bowed my head. After a short silence, he departed, but his gentle, compassionate demonstration of concern was etched in my memory.

Mother and I were alone. She turned to me and said, "Fran, you know that we want what is best for Jeffrey, and God knows what is best." We both cried. Through my tears, I haltingly whispered, "I know." In my spirit, God was preparing me for Jeffrey's death, but I still wanted my son to live.

It was difficult to call Jim and report the morning happenings. He made plans to drive from Greenville to Dallas as soon as possible. Mother and I moved to the ICU waiting room, which became our home for the next twenty-four hours. Our visitation time with Jeffrey was limited to five minutes every hour, so the remaining fifty-five minutes was spent in or near the waiting room. We waited for any report of a change in Jeffrey's condition.

On Wednesday afternoon a host of friends came from Greenville. Each time visitors arrived we stood, joined hands in a circle, and prayed. We took turns praying aloud and unashamedly for Jeffrey.

One friend, Harry, shared a verse that seemed so appropriate for the moment, 2 Corinthians 12:9: "My grace is sufficient for you." It was short and easy to remember. I said it over and over again to myself after he left. Eddie brought another thought from Isaiah 26:3: "Thou wilt keep him in perfect peace, whose mind is stayed on thee: because he trusteth in thee" (KJV).

I hurt so much for my son that the ordinary needs of life seemed mechanical. When someone said it was time to eat, they took me to the cafeteria. I tried to eat, but the lump in my throat made it difficult to swallow food. My stomach was in a knot. I understood the great possibility that Jeffrey might not live, but I was still clinging to hope.

Until this point, I had been so self-centered during Jeffrey's illness that I had failed to notice other parents who were also in agony over their children's condition. When we moved into the ICU waiting room, however, I became aware of a quiet, unassuming Latin-American lady sitting alone. After a brief introduction, Tony Sias shared that her infant son, Jesse, was in the intensive care unit with a serious heart abnormality. She and her husband had two daughters and had always longed for a little boy. Now her son was critically ill, and he had been sick since his birth. Mrs. Sias watched intently as our friends came and prayed with us. Johanna and Linda talked with her and gave her a Spanish New Testament.

Every parent in that waiting room shared a time of great pressure and uncertainty. We were not alone.

Wednesday afternoon, Jim and I felt it necessary to leave the hospital for just a breath of fresh air and emotional release from the prison of suspense. We needed to be alone, to reinforce our oneness of spirit. Sandy and Jim, friends for many years, offered their home as a refuge. Their sensitivity to our need was enhanced by their own previous experience in the death of an infant daughter. Their house was located only minutes away from the hospital, which allowed us to return within the allocated time and not miss the opportunity to be with Jeffrey for five minutes every hour.

We had been consumed by the oppressive atmosphere of the hospital. What a liberating change of pace to smell the fresh breeze and walk to the doorway of our brief retreat! Nothing could have been more welcome than a glass of cool lemonade, clean towels, and a quiet room. Sandy treated us like royalty.

As I rested in the serenity of this warm home, God spoke to my heart and told me that something good was going to happen to Jeffrey that night, and everything was going to be better for him. I did not understand those thoughts at all, but an overwhelming sense of peace prevailed.

Reluctantly, but refreshed, Jim and I returned to the

hospital. We did not talk much. We each feared we would have to say good-bye to our son, although we were not giving up hope that some miracle would happen to save him. I had never seen my husband weep, but that day he could no longer hold back the tears.

That evening our family accompanied us to the hospital cafeteria. That was when I noticed that the "knot" in my stomach had disappeared and I could eat without difficulty. I sensed an awareness of God's peace I could not explain. Somehow, God's grace had become more than just words. It was being translated into reality.

But through it all, Jeffrey's condition remained unchanged.

S I X
Transfer to Heaven

For we know that when this tent we live in now is taken down—when we die and leave these bodies—we will have wonderful new bodies in heaven, homes that will be ours forevermore, made for us by God himself, and not by human hands. 2 Corinthians 5:1, TLB

✷ At five o'clock Thursday morning I arose from the downstairs couch and rushed to the outer ICU door, hoping to catch the night nurse who took care of Jeffrey.

To my amazement, Johanna and David were sitting in the small room adjoining the hallway. They had driven again from Greenville early that morning just to be with us, to wait and pray. We talked until the nurse came out. She was surprised to see me.

I asked expectantly, "Can you tell me one good thing that happened to Jeffrey during the night?"

She had a ready answer. "Yes, there was one thing.

Prior to tonight, there had been a tremendous loss of body fluids due to damage to the pituitary gland. We do not understand why, but last night Jeffrey's urinary output significantly decreased. There has been no other change in his condition, though. I'm sorry."

God's impression the night before had proven true. My conversation with the night nurse confirmed that one good thing did occur to Jeffrey. Clinging to that thread of hope, I began the day with optimism.

Later that morning, the pediatric neurologist avoided me in the hallway. Apparently he had no good news to report. I ran after him and tugged on his arm, asking, "Have you seen Jeffrey this morning? Is he better?"

He somberly lowered his head and stated resolutely, "No change." Encouraged after talking with the night nurse, I could not help saying, "We still have hope!" From his expression, he must have thought I was unaware of the grave situation.

Jim and I both knew the problems involved, but we also knew that God had the power to resurrect during the darkest hour if it was in His plan to do so. We could not give up now.

Back in the ICU waiting room, friends had gathered. Again we prayed for specific signs of improvement. We prayed that the doctors taking care of Jeffrey would be encouraged. Fervently we said, "Dear God, please let Jeffrey live! Make him well and whole again." We also remembered the prayer Jesus prayed before facing the cross, and in recognition of the sovereignty of God we added, "Nevertheless, not our will be done, but Thine."

When Jeffrey was born, Jim and I had joined hearts in thanksgiving, realizing that he was a precious gift from God. Now we had to come to grips again with the fact that Jeffrey did indeed belong to God. We had to place him in God's care once and for all. We had loved him dearly for seventeen months, but we had to hand him to the heavenly Father in faith, trusting that He knew best.

It was almost noon when Dr. Hill and Dr. Brant approached Jim and me in the hallway and asked us to step into a private room nearby for a conference. Sadly, they explained that Jeffrey had not improved at all. The decreased urinary output during the night was not a significant factor in the turn of events. In fact, the respirator designed to support life seemed only a way of prolonging death because Jeffrey's brain activity had ceased. Jeffrey did not respond to treatment as they had hoped he might. The doctors wanted to prepare us, telling us there was no hope for our son's recovery.

Jim explained to them that we had prayed and believed God could intervene if it was His will to do so. We requested they monitor Jeffrey's condition carefully for a few more hours. The doctors were skeptical, but kindly agreed.

The pressure mounted and again Jim and I had to seek relief from the stressful situation. Together we returned to our friends' home early in the afternoon. While resting, I recalled the events of the day before. Reflecting upon the past hours, the thoughts God had planted in my mind Wednesday became clearer. Something good had happened to Jeffrey during the night, confirmed by the ICU nurse. Things *would* be better for Jeffrey. Now I knew why—because Jeffrey would be with Him! But how could I possibly let go? How I adored him! Then the answer came, "My grace is sufficient for you."

As we drove back to the hospital Jim and I both shed tears but said very little. Jim suggested we go straight to the chapel. A light over a stained-glass window gave the room a soft glow. Alone, we knelt at the altar in front of a cross and Jim voiced our prayer, "Dear God, we know that You love Jeffrey with a perfect love. We thank You for him and for allowing us to have him these seventeen months. We pray that this experience will be for our good and for Your glory. Thank You for entrusting us with this trial. Give us grace for what lies ahead."

It was difficult to move, but after a long embrace we made our way upstairs to say good-bye to our son.

Johanna was standing outside the door as Jim and I approached. I whispered in her ear, "I have peace."

Jim and I stood together beside Jeffrey. All the equipment was working—there were tubes, monitors, beeping sounds—but the natural was overpowered by the reality of the supernatural.

Angels were surely hovering around us. I sensed I could almost reach out and touch their wings. We felt an all-consuming peace as we held Jeffrey's hand and prayed with him, committing him to his Maker.

Our tears came not only from breaking human hearts but also from the joy of knowing that soon Jeffrey would behold the face of Jesus. He would be completely healed—safe forever.

But now he has died; why should I fast? Can I bring him back again? I shall go to him, but he will not return to me. 2 Samuel 12:23

SEVEN
Going Home

And we are not afraid, but are quite content to die, for then we will be at home with the Lord. 2 Corinthians 5:8, TLB

✳ That afternoon, the Lord took our youngest child into His presence. The reality of Jeffrey's departure was scary and lonely. As we looked at him for the last time, we knew his spirit was not there. His body was like an abandoned instrument, once making melody but now painfully silent. I felt confused. The days of stressful waiting were over. In a sense, I felt relief in knowing the outcome of the illness. On the other hand, the outcome brought with it disillusionment and disbelief. The last hope for Jeffrey's life was gone, and the finality of his death draped around my spirit like a black cape. The wretched emptiness and longing for his physical presence could only be expressed in tears.

I knew that others had walked in the valley because in Psalm 23:4 David said, "Yea, though I walk through the valley of the shadow of death, I will fear no evil: for thou art with me; thy rod and thy staff they comfort me" (KJV).

The comfort of God cannot be explained, only experienced. It is not an anesthetic to dull the pain, but it is supernatural strength to keep moving even though it hurts. In moments of turmoil and tears, I sensed His presence.

Jim encountered the same hollow feeling as I. During the drive home from Dallas, each of us silently attempted to digest the shock of the previous four days. It was dreadful to return without Jeffrey.

We tearfully greeted Steve, Angie, and Grandma Sandin, exchanging hugs and information. After a brief reunion, we retreated to our bedroom.

In the midst of his own grief, Jim was very attentive to me. Emotionally we clung to each other, trying to supply strength but also hoping to find refuge for weakness. The security of our relationship was a source of peace. That evening, the first without Jeffrey, we strongly felt the need to pray together. In great humility we knelt beside our bed. With wisdom that could only have come from the Holy Spirit, Jim voiced a prayer. "Lord, You know how we feel. The forces of evil would like to torment us with guilt and depression. I pray that You would overrule and bless us with a night of rest, which we so desperately need. Thank You, Father, for loving us. In Jesus' name, amen."

God answered our prayer. We awakened refreshed

and sought help in planning a memorial service that would be a celebration of life—not an anguishing over death. We recalled 1 Thessalonians 4:13-14: "But I would not have you to be ignorant, brethren, concerning them which are asleep, that ye sorrow not, even as others which have no hope. For if we believe that Jesus died and rose again, even so them also which sleep in Jesus will God bring with him" (KJV).

Saturday morning, May 4, 1974, was brilliant with sunshine. The earth was bursting forth with life. I was reminded of Easter Sunday when we rejoiced in the resurrection of our Lord and Savior, Jesus Christ. Without that event, we would have no hope of ever seeing Jeffrey or being with him again. But knowing that Jeffrey was alive with Jesus in heaven gave us hope amid the cloud of sorrow.

Before the memorial service began, we took Steve and Angie privately to say good-bye to Jeffrey. They had many questions. It was hard for them to understand that their little brother would no longer live in our home, but they accepted the explanation that Jeffrey was living with Jesus. That was the beginning of many conversations about a very real place—heaven.

The atmosphere of our church sanctuary was quiet, sweet, expectant. Grandparents, family members, and a host of friends joined in the worship service. The precious voices and innocent faces of the children's choir radiated praise to God as they sang, "Jesus Loves Me."

Another chorus they sang was "He's Got the Whole World in His Hands." This was very meaningful to our children because our family often sang this in the car when we traveled. As we sang we said each person's name and felt secure that God knew us individually. The lilting tune again reminded us that Jeffrey was indeed in His hands.

Indelible memories were made that day. Friends generously cared for my physical and emotional needs. Flowers covered the front of the church, representing people whose loving arms surrounded me and lifted my spirit. I needed each one.

I was amazed at the Father's loving touch. The poem printed on the memorial service bulletin was a favorite I'd memorized years ago but had since forgotten. When my eyes landed upon it, I heard Him whisper inside my heart, "Trust Me." This was the poem:

THE WEAVER

My life is but a weaving
Between my Lord and me,
I cannot choose the colors
He worketh steadily.

Ofttimes He weaveth sorrow,
And I in foolish pride
Forget He sees the upper
And I, the underside.

Not till the loom is silent
And the shuttles cease to fly
Shall God unroll the canvas
And explain the reason why.

The dark threads are as needful
　　　In the Weaver's skillful hand
As the threads of gold and silver
　　　In the pattern He has planned.

—Author Unknown

As the service ended, I realized God's finger was on my pulse. I was aware the Great Physician had placed me in His Intensive Care Unit. His celestial needle and thread were already mending my broken heart. His staff were caring family and friends on each side, holding me up as I began walking along the rugged road to recovery.

At home, in the stillness of the night, my desire to hold Jeffrey was intense. Tears trickled onto my pillow as I softly cried, "Jeffrey is gone. What must I do now, Lord?"

This Scripture came to mind: "I want you to trust me in your times of trouble, so I can rescue you, and you can give me glory" (Psalm 50:15, TLB).

EIGHT
Heaven: A Real Place

But as it is written, eye hath not seen, or ear heard, neither have entered into the heart of man, the things which God hath prepared for them that love him.
1 Corinthians 2:9, KJV

✳ I had not given heaven much thought until Jeffrey moved there. From that moment, it became a vitally important place. One evening, after a short family devotional time, the children asked detailed questions about their younger brother's new home.

"Will Jeffrey eat angel food cake all the time?" Steve wanted to know. Our vivacious kindergartner had a zest for yummy treats. During nightly prayer times, he thanked God for all the jelly beans and lollipops. Jim and I had to smile as we reassured him that whatever Jeffrey wanted or needed was being provided in abundance. Steve's eyes sparkled in response as he exclaimed,

"Wow!" We could just imagine what he was thinking.

Angie, our three-year-old, was curious, too. Obviously concerned, she asked, "Are there baby beds in heaven?" That was a new thought. What could I say? Jim and I made a few comments to indicate we could not answer many details about heaven because we did not know. However, we confirmed our belief that every single need was being met. Steve and Angie seemed satisfied and the conversation ended on a cheerful note.

Jim and I discussed with each other the inadequacy we felt in trying to explain heaven. A few months later, as we browsed through a Christian bookstore in Dallas, a colorful little book seemed to leap off the shelf and demand our attention. *If I Should Die, If I Should Live* was profound and appropriate to share with our children. It was so intriguing that I eagerly began reading it aloud to Jim as we drove back to Greenville. Its simple message was an encouragement to *us,* too. One passage in particular spoke to us:

Think of the most beautiful sight in the world. Heaven is even more beautiful . . . so beautiful no one can even imagine it!

Think of the happiest thing that could ever happen. Heaven is even happier . . . and no one will ever cry there!

Think of the most fun you could ever have. Heaven is more fun . . . and it will last forever![1]

Isn't that fantastic! During the days of emotional stress, I tried to concentrate upon the reality of heaven. I found that when I dwelt in my sorrow and loss I became depressed. Just the opposite was true when I thought about heaven. The very idea of such a wonderfully indescribable place lightened my spirits and made my heart sing. I began to realize that all of the beauty, goodness, and love we experience while on earth is but a brief peep through the keyhole to all that awaits us in heaven. I envisioned Jeffrey being cuddled in the strong, loving arms of Jesus, having perfect fellowship with Grandpa Sandin and others he had never met. I paused to "rethink" Jeffrey's death. Although it was called a tragedy, I wondered what could be so terrible about being loved and nurtured in the safest, most wonderful home of all?

Contemplating heaven took out some of the "sting of death." Knowing that someday Jeffrey and I would be reunited forever gave me peace.

The knowledge of heaven did not remove all tears, however. I cried most often at night when everything was quiet and touching memories came to mind. At other times, tears were unpredictable . . . the sight of a toddler Jeffrey's size, a hymn at church that expressed God's faithfulness, the understanding expression on the face of a compassionate friend all could start me crying. But God made our eyes with tear ducts, and he gave us the capacity for deeply felt emotions. God knows how it feels to hurt. John 11:35 says, "Jesus wept." God knows everything about us. He notices when we cry. He even keeps track of our tears, according to Psalm 56:8: "Thou hast taken account of my wanderings; put my tears in Thy bottle; are they not in Thy book?"

Those who love God can know that some day we will experience the precious promise of Revelation 7:17, which says, "God shall wipe every tear from their eyes."

As fellow believers ministered to us during Jeffrey's illness and death, I knew I had tasted a bit of heaven's glory. Their acts of love, kindness, and unselfish abandon visually aided the panorama of wonderful fellowship, harmony, and freedom we can anticipate in heaven. In heaven we will experience oneness of spirit, all in one accord. All barriers will be broken. What a great day that will be!

Yes, there is a real place called heaven, reserved for those who place their faith and trust in Jesus Christ as Lord and Savior. "For God so loved the world [you and me], that He gave His only begotten Son, that whoever believes in Him should not perish, but have eternal life" (John 3:16).

If I had not known that someday I would see Jeffrey again, the pain of his departure would have been too great to bear. Now I find thoughts of heaven a pleasant reminder that my family has a little treasure there and soon we will be together forever.

I enjoyed learning and singing this little chorus:

> *Heaven is a wonderful place—*
> *filled with glory and grace,*
> *I want to see my Savior's face;*
> *Heaven is a wonderful place.*

N I N E
Is God Punishing Me?

Even when we are too weak to have any faith left, he remains faithful to us and will help us, for he cannot disown us who are part of himself, and he will always carry out his promises to us. 2 Timothy 2:13, TLB

✳ The house was quiet. The children were asleep, and Jim was at work. I sat alone at the kitchen table, plagued with questions that had crossed my mind for several weeks. If I had called the doctor sooner, would Jeffrey have lived? The week before he became ill I had taken Jeffrey with me while running some errands. If only I had left him at home . . . would he have escaped the seemingly unexplainable illness? While pondering and searching for answers, I wondered again and again if Jeffrey's death was due to God's disapproval of something I had done.

Perhaps God was chastening me for some foolish remark. Once while chatting with my sister I said flippantly, "I was so surprised when Jeffrey was born. Instead of a boy I was expecting a dark-haired, brown-eyed girl." As I reflected upon this conversation, I wondered if God was unhappy with me for making that comment. Had I seemed ungrateful for our son? Surely not. Jeffrey was a beautiful, blond-haired, blue-eyed, healthy baby, and I loved him deeply.

Maybe God was correcting me for my failures as a mother. I knew I had made mistakes. While I had never knowingly or intentionally harmed the children, occasionally I had reacted with anger and impatience.

I reflected upon one day in particular when exhaustion compelled me to take an afternoon nap. Our three preschoolers were tucked into their beds, too; but just as I completely relaxed and closed my eyes, Steve and Jeffrey began making noises. They were getting in and out of bed in spite of my instructions to the contrary.

Exasperated, I grabbed the "rod of correction" and, on short notice, paddled them both. Recalling that event, I thought about the surprised look on Jeffrey's face as big tears rolled down his cheeks. He had cried and cried. Had I overreacted?

Then I had to remind myself that God instructs us as parents to discipline our children. Even if I failed in some way that day, the ultimate goal was to teach obedience. Surely God knew my heart.

After a time of silent meditation there at the kitchen table, I looked up and caught a glimpse of a booklet on the counter. I reached over, opened it, and began reading. *Death of a Little Child* by J. Vernon McGee offered this paragraph to comfort me.

Perhaps you are rebuking yourself for not having done something more in behalf of the child. You may be harassed by a haunting fear that you did something wrong. Martha and Mary felt that the death of their brother could have been averted. They both said to Him, "Lord, if thou hadst been here my brother would not have died" (John 11:21, 32). Yet in the providence of God it was best for Lazarus to die, though it could have been averted—but only with divine help. Humanly speaking, you did the best you could. You are not as wise nor as strong as God. You did what you could, and you must leave the results to Him. Do not reproach yourself for negligence or ignorance. Regardless of what you had done, you are still a fallible and feeble creature. You did the best you could.[2]

The words reassured me, but still I was not satisfied. A new door of nagging doubt opened. I began to recall sins of my past. Like a television rerun they paraded across my mind, and their remembrance was painful. Could it be that Jeffrey's death was God's punishment for my past sins?

A few weeks later, as I attended a Bible study, I was amazed to read that a woman in Scripture had asked the same question. In 1 Kings 17:18, a widow cried to the prophet, asking, "O man of God . . . what have you done to me? Have you come here to punish my sins by killing my son?" (TLB). Her poignant cry revealed her acute awareness of sin. I identified with her.

However, within minutes a different thought emerged. Even though I felt a sense of shame for my sins, I knew that I had prayed and asked forgiveness according to 1 John 1:9, "If we confess our sins, He is faithful and righteous to forgive us our sins and to cleanse us from all unrighteousness." I began to realize that if God had forgiven me, I must forgive myself. Otherwise I would not be acting upon God's personal word to me.

Divine guidance seemed at work a couple of days later when my dear friend Linda brought me a magazine that featured the following verses in bold type, occupying an entire page of the publication:

The LORD is merciful and gracious, slow to anger, and plenteous in mercy. He will not always chide: neither will he keep his anger for ever. He hath not dealt with us after our sins; nor rewarded us according to our iniquities. For as the heaven is high above the earth, so great is his mercy toward them that fear him. As far as the east is from the west, so far hath he removed our transgressions from us. Like as a father pitieth his children, so the Lord pitieth them that fear him. For he knoweth our frame; he remembereth that we are dust. " Psalm 103:8-14, KJV

For a time, it was difficult for me to feel forgiven, although I knew it was true. I even began thinking of small regrets—things I wished I had done for Jeffrey, like having a professional photograph made just of him.

In his tender way, the Lord addressed my concerns through the pages of a book about grief. The author observed that often after the death of a loved one we pile up a huge stack of regrets. We remember what we did that we should not have done; we reconstruct everything we wish we had done. Our heartache intensifies as we suffer through remorseful feelings and guilt. We relive old conflicts if there were any. Responding to these natural tendencies, the author concluded that true healing comes when we accept God's forgiveness and throw away the burden of regret.[3]

Our heavenly Father had graciously reassured my questioning heart concerning foolish remarks, failures as a mother, past sins, and regrets, but He seemed to know how much I needed one final word of encouragement.

It came one Sunday evening as my husband and I listened to a visiting pastor in our local church. As part of his message, he said, "No pain or sorrow that comes to us could be severe enough to punish us for our sins. Sin (falling short of God's moral standards) is so contrary to God that it required the blood of Jesus Christ, His Son, perfect and blameless, to cover the sin of all mankind— once and for all. We must confess our sins and accept his forgiveness."

Continuing, he added, "If we receive Christ into our hearts, accept His forgiveness, and become God's child, then nothing can happen to us that He does not allow. God is interested in how we react to our trials. If we hand Him the pieces of our broken hearts and broken lives, He can take them and make them beautiful."

At that moment I could think of nothing more devastating than Jeffrey's death, and no one more precious than my Lord and Savior, Jesus Christ. I know that in order to get on with normal, healthy living I must leave everything in His forgiving hands and trust Him for tomorrow.

Is God punishing me? was a question I could not talk about with anyone except God, but He is the best counselor I know. It took a number of months for me to work through the self-condemnation I experienced after Jeffrey's illness and death. Through the truth I found in God's Word, and the messengers He sent, I learned to leave the questioning behind.

God is faithful. He does make all things beautiful . . . in His time. Assured of His love, mercy, and forgiveness, I began searching for the productive life He designed just for me.

T E N
How Can I Conquer Fear?

He will cover you with His feathers, and under His wings you will find refuge. Psalm 91:4, NIV

❋ One night after an evening meal, Angie sighed, "I wish I could sit on Jesus' lap. He would tell me a story." Steve chimed in with, "Yeah, Jeffrey is really lucky *he* can be with Jesus." Jim and I were grateful for each good attitude. However, my first thought was, *Please do not wish to be with Jesus* now! The very idea of anyone else leaving was devastating. My introspection ceased, however, as I heard Jim explaining gently, "God is very wise. *He* will decide the right time for us to go to heaven."

Jeffrey's death strongly affected each family member. I was so fearful for the children's safety that I cancelled their summer swimming lessons. When Angie became ill with a viral infection, the first reading on the thermometer indicated a slight temperature elevation. Jim and I rushed her to the doctor. No antibiotics were required; it was a short illness. Nevertheless, we were shaken and had overreacted.

A few months later, Jim developed bronchitis during a family vacation. He became very weak. In fact, he stayed in bed. The children had never seen their dad incapacitated for any reason. Steve wanted to know, "Mommy, is Daddy going to die?" Prior to Jeffrey's death, I might have casually answered, "Of course not." Now, to my sensitive and frightened son, I could only say, "Let's pray that Daddy will get well soon." As I hugged Steve and prayed, my voice cracked; my arms and my stomach quivered. I felt the same uncertainty as he. In a few days, Daddy recovered. We all rejoiced.

It is not uncommon for people experiencing grief to be emotionally depleted. I recognized in myself a greater tendency to be fearful and worried, sometimes even discouraged without a good cause. Yet I did not want to be consumed with fear. What could I do?

Through reading helpful books, I learned to find a balance. Worry or fear need not paralyze us, but neither should we go through life with a lack of concern for those we love.

In his book *Overcoming Anxiety* Gary R. Collins states,

Psychology and the Bible both agree that there is nothing wrong with being concerned about the problems of life. Indeed, this is really very healthy, especially when the concern is focused upon the needs and wel-

fare of others. But the Bible and psychology also agree that to take a blasé attitude or to be immobilized by excessive worry is also unhealthy. When this happens, we should be willing to honestly look at why we feel as we do, seeking, when necessary, the help of a Christian friend or counselor. In all of this we must trust in Christ to help us with the problem or anxiety as He has promised.[4]

I knew, intellectually at least, that Christ promised to help me overcome anxiety. But how?

One day as I was cleaning house I remembered that in the past when a problem was burdensome it was comforting to meditate upon Scripture related to the subject. Locating some passages regarding fear, I laid the Bible open on the kitchen table. It was handy for reference as I memorized verses.

One of my favorites was Psalm 56:3, "When I am afraid, I will put my trust in Thee." Another was Isaiah 41:10, "Do not fear, for I am with you; do not anxiously look about you, for I am your God. I will strengthen you, surely I will help you, surely I will uphold you with My righteous right hand."

The exercise of memorizing and repeating verses aloud helped me to feel that Christ cared for me personally. He seemed very near.

On another occasion I was reading Matthew 14. A description of fear caught my attention. Peter walked on water at Jesus' command until he looked aside and saw the high waves and wind. He became afraid and began to sink. He cried out, "Lord, save me!" Jesus reached out and took hold of him. When they climbed back into the boat, the wind stopped. The other disciples in the boat were amazed. They exclaimed, "You, Jesus, really are the Son of God!"

The comment Jesus made to Peter as He reached for him was, "O you of little faith, why did you doubt?" (vv. 28-33).

Walking on water is certainly not the "natural" thing to do. Peter was an ordinary man, incapable of such an act. Jesus supernaturally endowed him with power. When did Peter start sinking? When he forgot the all-sufficiency of Jesus Christ and looked around at the frightening circumstances of the moment. Did Jesus leave him when he cried out for help? No. He reached out and rescued Peter from danger.

What an interesting account. Even the disciples were afraid at times. Jesus understood their fear and reached out to help them. This story reminded me that Jesus is always present. Regardless of the circumstances around me, I must keep my eyes upon Him.

Another principle I learned through further study is that fear is not wrong. God designed us with healthy emotions; fear is one of them. For example, our fear of danger enables us to take necessary safety precautions.

The Scriptures even describe the fear of God as a "healthy" fear. Why should man fear God? Because He is the Creator, the all-powerful, all-knowing God of the universe, the One whom we as His children desire to obey. We shouldn't be afraid of Him in the sense that we would fear a malevolent dictator; nevertheless, we stand in reverence and awe of Him.

Oddly enough, only through fearing God can man receive the comfort God desires to give. God's perfect love, manifested through Jesus Christ, casts away fear and allows us to rest under the sheltering wings of His sovereignty. Author Jay Adams wrote,

Love is self-giving; fear is self-protecting. Love moves toward others; fear shrinks away from them. But . . . love is the stronger since it is able to 'cast out' fear. In dealing with fear, nothing else possesses the same expulsive power.

Although under other circumstances she might be frightened by a mouse, a mother is not immobilized by the fear of a wild animal attacking the child that she loves. Foolishly or otherwise, her love overcomes fear and casts it out as she throws herself into the fray. Love thus demonstrates itself as greater.[5]

Growth in love produces a boldness or confidence in us as we approach our heavenly Father. The more closely we walk with Him, the less fear and the more confidence we have in coming before Him.

Isn't it interesting to note that in the Scriptures Jesus is never said to be afraid? The obvious reason for this was that His love was perfect.[6]

After Jeffrey's death, my natural response to the pain of grief was fear, namely that another tragedy would happen. My broken, tender heart could not bear another blow. In the days that followed, it helped me to make Scripture promises personal, to remember Christ's presence, and to learn more of God's character and His ways. These factors increased my trust in Him. However, it also exposed my own selfish desire to be in "control" of my family's well-being.

My real liberation from this gripping fear came the day I realized I had to "let go" of my family and entrust them to His care. I did this through a prayer.

Dear Lord, I give each member of my family to You. I am sure You love them with a perfect love. Since You have greater knowledge of their needs, I know I can trust You to watch over them. Whatever happens, I acknowledge that You are sovereign, and You are in control.

Since that day, I have felt reassured that I do not have to fear the future because *God is already there.* I have learned the truth of Psalm 94:19: "When my anxious thoughts multiply within me, Thy consolations delight my soul."

ELEVEN
Will I Ever Get Over This?

When Thou didst say, "Seek My face," my heart said to Thee, "Thy face, O LORD, I shall seek." Psalm 27:8

✳ "There, it's finished!" I stood back and admired the étagère in our living room, four shelves in a lighted, glassed case. The past hour, I had carefully arranged momentos on each shelf . . . Jeffrey's picture, his two-toned walking shoes, a piggy bank engraved with his name, his Bible, favorite toys, spoon and fork, and other special possessions of his. I felt relieved to gather all his belongings in one place. But I would rather have had him! I daydreamed about his presence. Visual contact with his things made me feel I could hear him or touch him. I wished he would surprise me and walk through the door.

The week after Jeffrey died I took Steve and Angie to "Mother's Day Out" as usual. Automatically I pulled three lunch boxes from the kitchen cabinet and began packing snacks. I was halfway through the third when I remembered that Jeffrey wouldn't need his. I thought about the last time Jeffrey went with us; of his exuberance as he waved good-bye through the nursery window. His smile was imprinted there on the glass. As we drove up, I saw it. Tearfully, I trudged into the church with the children and their paraphernalia. The workers greeted me with hugs and sympathy; the nostalgia was overwhelming. Jim and I met later for lunch. He encouraged me. Without him, I could not have made it through that day.

At home, I moved through my daily tasks like a robot. I seldom concentrated upon the task at hand. The children perceived my preoccupation with memories. One day Steve's small voice jolted me as he inquired, "Mommy, do you really love me?" Did I? Of course! More than words could say! I was crushed that he asked. He needed my affection and undivided attention. I stopped working, sat in the big chair, and lifted him into my lap for a time of hugging, kissing, and rocking. It was good for both of us.

The first year passed. Each holiday, birthday, or special event was a painful reminder of Jeffrey's absence. At times during the year I experienced brief episodes of physical pain around my heart. While I had no history of heart disease in my family, I did go to the doctor for some tests, which were negative. Eventually, the genuine heartache of grief subsided.

During the second year I attended a Christian women's meeting. The speaker was a young mother who gave a testimony about God's faithfulness to her through widowhood. She related that after the passing of time, the Lord impressed upon her the need to behold the future. In essence, the message was, "The portion of your life spent with your husband was good and wonderful. Now you must seek *My* face and *My* plans for you. Stop looking back! Start looking ahead!"

Those words hit me like a dash of cold water! *Fran, that message is for you.* After the meeting, I promptly departed and drove to the cemetery. A visit to Jeffrey's grave was rare because I knew he wasn't there—he was in heaven with Jesus. But at that particular time, I had to go. It was the only place I knew I could weep alone, no questions asked. The grounds were deserted. I stood by the marker and cried awhile, then drove home, resolved to do what the Lord had inspired. With determination, I steadfastly walked into the living room, opened the étagère, and removed everything. I placed all of Jeffrey's keepsakes in the cedar chest. By the time Jim came home I had redecorated the shelves with brightly colored dishes and vases. Lightheartedly, I met him at the door, grasped his hand, and led him to see the metamorphosis. He was so happy! He secretly knew my forward progress was being hindered, but he was also aware that vocal disapproval would have appeared harsh. God is so good, so gentle. In His own timing, He helped *me* decide to change!

A few months later it was a joy to give Jeffrey's clothes to a couple going on an out-of-state mission trip. His clothing was distributed to little boys in needy families.

I felt I was moving slowly in the right direction but often felt a tug of self-pity. Then one day I read with interest the scriptural account of David's grief in 2 Samuel 12.

During the illness of his infant son, David fasted, prayed, and pleaded with God to spare his child. But on the seventh day Bathsheba's baby died. David's aides had observed his behavior during the infant's illness, and when the child died, they were afraid to tell him for fear of his response. When David saw them whispering, he guessed what had happened. However, to their amazement, David arose, took a bath, changed his clothes, brushed his hair, went into the Tabernacle, and worshiped the Lord. Then he went to the palace and ate.

His aides were bewildered. They asked David about his behavior, and he replied, "I fasted and wept while the child was alive, for I said, 'Perhaps the Lord will be gracious to me and let the child live.' But why should I fast when he is dead? Can I bring him back again? *I shall go to him, but he shall not return to me*" (vv. 22-23, TLB).

Instead of weeping at the grave and hanging onto his sorrow, he looked toward the glory in which his child would be waiting. Then he pressed forward into his responsibilities.

David's story reminded me of a living example in my own experience. My grandmother, whom I affectionately called "Ma," was not a trained psychologist, but she knew the principle that work is a good antidote for depression. After my grandfather's death, I watched as she continued to care for the farm, feed the animals, hoe the garden, and minister to her friends. She didn't sit around feeling sorry for herself.

As I recalled those days, I realized that she met the untimely and unexpected death of her mate with courage. Then she persevered in the goals they had planned together. I do not remember ever hearing Ma complain. What a beautiful example she was. I knew she loved my grandfather dearly and missed him immensely, but she left her sorrow behind and proceeded to live a productive, meaningful life.

God must have brought these illustrations to my attention to help me realize another of His precious lessons. At a certain point, normal grief merges into self-pity. If that occurs, one feels little desire to help others because all energy is focused upon oneself. I found that by making a conscious effort to do something for someone else, I spent less time thinking of my hurt. It was very therapeutic.

For instance, I was sentimental about special days. When Jeffrey's birthday came and he was not with us, I decided to give presents to friends who had unselfishly cared for our family. I scurried off to the local florist and bought a fistful of fresh flowers. At home, I gave Angie a quick course in arrangements. We worked together making several bouquets. They were not prizewinners, but each was sprinkled with lots of tender loving care. Steve helped with deliveries. What a delightful afternoon we had, as the children and I shared Jeffrey's birthday with others.

Plowing through grief was a matter of self-discipline.

As God showed me how to move forward in His time, I moved. Sometimes the message came from Scripture, a tape, a friend, a book, a speaker. Had I waited for my feelings to change first, I would not have acted. It was easier to mope. God showed me He was ready to do His part for progress. I had to do mine.

J. R. Miller wrote in *Words of Comfort:*

Grief should always make us better and give us new skill and power; it should make our heart softer, our spirit kindlier, our touch more gentle; it should teach us its holy lessons, and we should learn them, and then go on, with sorrow's sacred ordination upon us, to new love and better service. It is thus, too, that lonely hearts find their sweetest, richest comfort. Sitting down to brood over our sorrows, the darkness deepens about us and our little strength changes to weakness; but if we turn away from the gloom and take up the tasks of comforting and helping others, the light will come again and we shall grow strong.[7]

The answer to "Will I ever get over this?" is that with God's help, I must. It will be easier if I thank Him for the beautiful memories, persevere in finding His plan for my future, and spend time serving others. "Delight yourself in the LORD; and He will give you the desires of your heart" (Psalm 37:4).

T W E L V E
Should We Adopt?

If any of you lacks wisdom, let him ask of God, who gives to all men generously and without reproach, and it will be given to him. James 1:5

❋ *Dear Lord, it's me again. You are teaching me so much. Thanks for Your patience. There is just one thing. What are we going to do about this big, empty spot in my heart? No matter how much You love me, it still hurts. I've been staying busy, but I was just wondering—could it be that some little orphan baby needs a loving home? How about twins? On second thought—I'll just ask for one. Don't you think this is a terrific idea? Nothing is too hard for You! I will get some applications ready for the adoption agencies right away. Jim has no objections. Oh, isn't this exciting? I'm sure we will hear something soon. Thanks, heavenly Father.*

P.S. Oh, yes, remember, I gave Jeffrey's clothes away for missions —don't You think that was a nice thing to do? In case You may have forgotten, here is a verse— Luke 6:38: "Give, and it will be given to you; good measure, pressed down, shaken together, running over, they will pour into your lap." In Jesus' name, amen!

That was my presumptuous prayer. I thought surely God would not have allowed Jeffrey to die without having another child set aside for us. He knew how much I loved babies. After two years of searching for possibilities without any encouragement, I asked a rather pertinent question: "God, is it *Your* will for us to have another child?"

Gradually, I realized I was spending entirely too much time daydreaming about adoption. It was an emotional issue. I felt frustrated and desperate to know God's will. Finally, I decided to set aside one day each week for fasting and prayer concerning this matter. Jim was the only one who knew. My intention was to become spiritually alert; to release my motherly desires and be willing to accept God's answer, whatever it might be. In accordance with Psalm 35:13, "I humbled my soul with fasting."

After six months, a definite answer came. One of the contacts we had made regarding adoption called. He said, "There is a chance that a baby will be available to you within twenty-four to forty-eight hours. However, it's still uncertain at this time. I just wanted you to know, and I'll call back tomorrow."

At first, Jim and I were very excited. Later in the

evening, we sat in the family room and began dealing with this possibility as never before. As much as I had daydreamed, the idea of another child seemed remote until now. A frank, realistic discussion opened new channels in my thinking. Would this be best for Steve and Angie?

Jim was very communicative and discerning. He gently led me to recognize that my desire to adopt another baby was an unconscious desire to replace Jeffrey. As soon as he said it in words, its truth was confirmed in my heart. But I could never replace Jeffrey. Another baby could not meet my expectations. After a genuine exchange of ideas and prayer, God's answer to me regarding adoption was revealed through a loving and understanding husband. Six months before, I would have rebelled. Now I was ready to face the fact that adoption would not be wise for us at this time. I thanked the Lord for his tender, loving care.

The next day the telephone rang. It was the man who had contacted us before. "I am so sorry about this," he began, "but the baby I told you about will not be available after all. I hope you will not be too disappointed by this news. Please forgive any inconvenience it might have caused," he apologized. I thanked him, then I hung up the phone and rejoiced. I was released from bondage! God was faithful to accomplish what concerned me.

A beautiful message was whispered in my spirit as I contemplated a newly made family picture: "This is your family. Be glad. Do not seek after what you do not have. Be grateful for what I (the Lord) have given you.

Your fulfillment will be complete as you love and minister to each one." My husband and children became extremely precious. I prayed I would never forget the depth of perception He gave me in that moment. I knew my love for them would never be the same. It was already greater then ever before.

What about the empty spot? Soon after the adoption question had been answered, I went to a women's prayer group. Because it was near Christmas, we were having a birthday party for Jesus. Our leader, Mable, had taken quotations that represented "gifts" and wrapped each piece of paper in a small, decorated box. After our prayer time we each took a box—not knowing its contents—opened it, and read the enclosed quotation. We knelt beside the coffee table in Mable's home. It represented a little altar upon which we gave to Jesus our gift. In case you suspect God is too busy for small details, this was the paper I read as my gift:

A ray of light falling on a prism is broken up into many colors. In like manner, thank You, dear Father, that in Jesus You were revealing the various depths, hues, colors, and dimensions of Yourself, so that we, the human race, could understand and know You. I give to You a "new" goal for my life. I truly want God . . . not joy and peace and blessings . . . but Him—filling me up.

At times not one person on earth can meet the deepest needs of our lives. Only God can.

THIRTEEN
Does God Answer Prayer?

And in the same way the Spirit also helps our weakness; for we do not know how to pray as we should, but the Spirit Himself intercedes for us with groanings too deep for words. Romans 8:26

✳ *Why, God, why? Why didn't You heal Jeffrey of his illness? I wanted him to get well so he would be with us to grow up as part of our family. He brought us so much joy and now he's gone. Was all our praying to no avail? Did we lack enough faith? Didn't You hear?*

These questions began to haunt me several weeks after Jeffrey's death. The finality of his absence was painful. I knew God had given me peace, that He had been faithful to minister to my family's needs, but now I began to question the efficacy of prayer.

As long as I could remember, prayer had been an important part of my life. However, after Jeffrey's death,

I felt troubled, discouraged, empty, disillusioned. At that point it was not anger that I felt, but extreme disappointment.

In the depths of grief, I barely had the emotional strength to contend with my heavenly Father. But at one point, I felt I could not wait another day for some answers. When cards arrived from friends who wrote, *We're praying for you,* I thought, *That's good because I'm too weak to pray.*

One reason for my focus upon "unanswered prayer" was an incident that occurred during Jeffrey's illness. Allen, a kind and sincere friend, had come to Jim and me and quoted Matthew 18:19, "If two of you agree on earth about anything that they may ask, it shall be done for them by My Father who is in heaven." Our friend explained, "If only you have enough faith when you pray, your son will be healed."

That statement was difficult for us to accept. We were brokenhearted and helpless. We had faith, but we knew it was not our own. Our Lord had placed it within us. As we pondered that statement, we realized that even though many people had prayed diligently and specifically for Jeffrey, who in addition was receiving the benefit of modern medical techniques and medications, the doctors could discern no apparent improvement. We could see with our own eyes that he was not responding.

Allen's well-meaning admonition waved a banner of false hope over our dying child and placed the responsibility upon us as parents for the outcome of his illness. We were extremely concerned. We had already undergone a critical self-examination, and if anything in our hearts or lives might have hindered God's positive answer, we were not aware of it.

Jim and I recognized that Jeffrey belonged to God. We understood that God, if He had willed it, could have healed him instantly. Yet in the months following Jeffrey's death, the question haunted me. Did our son die because we lacked faith?

In my search for an answer, the Lord graciously brought some thoughts to my attention. First of all, Scripture contains balancing principles. Alongside the prayer promises are requirements to be met. First John 5:14 says, "If we ask anything *according to His will,* He hears us."

At the hospital, when Jeffrey's future was uncertain, I kept remembering Jesus as He prayed before the crucifixion, "My Father, if it is possible, let this cup pass from Me; yet not as I will, but as Thou wilt" (Matthew 26:39). The spirit of Christ was submissive. He did not tell God what to do. Although I wanted Jeffrey to live more than anything else in the world, I didn't feel comfortable trying to twist God's arm to answer my prayer in my way.

God exists as an all-knowing, all-powerful Being who knows both the spoken and unspoken needs of the heart. I believed He knew my longings; in my supplications, I knew that Jesus Himself, who had agonized through a life-and-death situation, was interceding for me at the Father's right hand.

I wanted to believe God would heal our son, but I left the final decision to His Sovereign will. Later, after Jeffrey's death, I read R. C. Sproul's comment on this issue in his book *Effective Prayer:*

Prayer is not magic. God is not a celestial bellhop ready at our beck and call to satisfy our every whim. In some cases our prayers must involve travail of the soul and agony of heart such as Jesus Himself experienced in the Garden. Sometimes the immature Christian suffers bitter disappointment, not because God failed to keep His promises, but because well-meaning Christians made promises "for" God that God Himself never authorized.[8]

Reading this confirmed my concern about the danger of isolating short prayer promises out of the context of the entire counsel of Scripture. Even though it was a frustrating experience at the time, our encounter with Allen caused me to read and study more about prayer.

Turning to Scripture, I found numerous prayers answered and many miracles described. But I also discovered that three of God's choicest servants experienced occasions when their prayers were not answered in the way they requested. Moses prayed that he might see Canaan after leading his people through the wilderness. He died without seeing it. At one point Elijah was deeply depressed and asked God to let him die. He lived. Paul suffered from some unknown affliction, and he asked God three times to remove it. But God didn't.[9]

In each case, God answered prayer in a different way. Moses did see Canaan, but from a new perspective— from heaven. Elijah left the earth in a much more exciting way than dying under a juniper tree! And Paul's thorn in the flesh has blessed literally millions of believers through the centuries, as we've understood the Lord's answer, "My grace is sufficient for you" (2 Corinthians 12:9).

Samuel Chadwick wrote, "No inspired prayer of faith is ever refused. 'No' is never God's last word. If the prayer seems unanswered, it is because it is lost in the glory of the answer when it comes. God may refuse the route because He knows a better way."[10]

I actually felt excited as I thought about the prayer of Jesus. If He had not undergone the Crucifixion, there could have been no Resurrection. Without the Resurrection, I would have no hope of ever seeing Jeffrey again. As I thought of the wonderful reunion we will have in Eternity I could only bow in humble adoration to a loving God whose knowledge of the past, present, and future affords perfect wisdom as He interprets our prayers.

Although we live in an imperfect world with imperfect bodies, God is still in control. He can and does, at times, overrule the natural course of events. We praise Him for this when it happens, and we call it a miracle.

Miracles also occur in the hearts of those who discover that God can use even heartaches and disappointments for their benefit. This happened to me as I studied about prayer.

God was patient, allowing me to learn afresh that prayer involves not only talking to Him but listening to Him speak to me. Prayer engages me in spiritual battle against the evil forces of the world. Prayer aligns my self with the Lord Jesus Christ and His desires for my life.

I learned that I am God's responsibility, and He is the great I AM. Whatever I need, He says, "I AM." He will never put me in a place without taking care of me. God does not forsake those who trust Him.

Prayer gives me an opportunity to thank and praise God, acknowledging His holiness, a time to listen to His instructions for daily living, a time to glorify Him. Rosalind Rinker once said, "Prayer is a dialogue between two persons who love each other."[11]

As a result of my study, two passages in particular took on new meaning. The first was Philippians 4:6-7, "Be anxious for nothing, but in everything by prayer and supplication with thanksgiving let your requests be made known to God. And the peace of God, which surpasses all comprehension, shall guard your hearts and your minds in Christ Jesus." I realized that my responsibility was to pray and leave the results with God.

The second grabbed my heart. First Thessalonians 5:18 reads, "In everything give thanks; for this is God's will for you in Christ Jesus." One day when the Holy Spirit brought this verse to my remembrance I literally stopped my work at home, sat down, and wept. I confessed to God that I didn't understand why Jeffrey died, but I expressed thanks—not with my emotions, but with my will—acknowledging that He is in control, and for whatever reason I could not understand, He allowed it to happen.

Through this expression of confidence in His sovereignty I gained freedom and release. My struggle to overcome disappointment about seemingly "unanswered prayer" was over. I felt God knew me intimately and knew my deepest desires. He embraced me with His love.

At last I understood that God did answer my prayer for Jeffrey, but in a different way. I found it beautifully expressed in Psalm 21:4: "He asked life of thee, and thou gavest it him, even length of days for ever and ever" (KJV).

F O U R T E E N
Am I Becoming Bitter?

See to it that no one comes short of the grace of God;
that no root of bitterness springing up causes trouble,
and by it many be defiled. Hebrews 12:15

✳ A few months after Jeffrey's death, my friend Marjorie visited in our home. During our conversation, she shared this warning: "Fran, be careful. Guard your heart. Do not be bitter toward God for what has happened. The first ones to be affected would be your own family, especially the children. You could cause them to turn against God also."

Marjorie then prayed a prayer for God's protection over my thought life. This powerful prayer caused me to desire God's grace for every new day. Her concern, encouragement, and prayers helped me to resist bitterness.

Through this special friend, God was teaching me

another lesson. When trials come, people are tempted to respond in a non-Biblical way with bitterness toward God for what has happened. When this caustic response takes root in a person's heart, it cannot be concealed. I later met Ginger, who illustrated this truth.

Ginger's teenaged son was killed in a car accident. When I visited her some months later, it became apparent that she was blaming God. As she wrung her hands, she made these statements: "If God really loved me, He would never have let this happen. I used to think God loved me, but now I do not know."

Ginger professed to be a Christian, but she seemed defeated. Her countenance was negative, harsh, and cold. Feelings of God's total abandonment must have consumed her, causing her to be insensitive to friends who offered assistance. The focus of her life at that point could be expressed in her own words, "God really let me down."

As I talked with Ginger, I felt pity for her. I could certainly understand her yearning for her son. In fact, emptiness and longing for Jeffrey were still very fresh in my own heart. But the barrier of bitterness Ginger erected was difficult to penetrate. I tried to help her think of something for which she could be thankful. The conversation seemed fruitless at the time, but I prayed she would accept God's grace.

As I reflected on that visit, I began to think more about God's grace and the consequences of rejecting it. Divine grace is undeserved mercy or favor. God gives us the appropriate measure when we need it. Grace is God giving us the power to do what is right. As God's children, we know that His grace is sufficient for every trial.

In *The Hiding Place,* Corrie ten Boom describes taking a train ride. She said her father always waited to give her the ticket. Just before she stepped on the train, he placed the ticket in her hand.[12] In the same way, our heavenly Father gives us grace when we need it—not sooner, not later, but just at the right time. We make a choice to either accept it or reject it.

As I struggled through grief I again recalled my beloved grandmother. She endured painful arthritis, bouts with heart problems, and the death of her husband, but she continued to love God relentlessly. I thought of my mother, a beautiful woman with a quiet and gentle spirit. She always taught me that God could use any situation in my life for good if I allowed Him to take control. Mother and Ma were living illustrations of a trusting response to God in all things. I had taken these observations lightly in earlier years, but during my own devastation, I drew upon the faith of these two special women to strengthen my reliance upon God. Accepting God's grace became easier as I recalled His faithfulness to them.

"This I recall to my mind, therefore I have hope. The LORD's lovingkindnesses indeed never cease, for His compassions never fail. They are new every morning; great is Thy faithfulness" (Lamentations 3:21-23).

Why did Jeffrey die? Why did I see others in tragic situations? During the time I was asking God I searched the Scriptures. After a great deal of study, some conclusions were helpful to me.

Death was not God's original plan for us. God created man for life—body, soul, and spirit. When sin entered the world, tragedy and death were its ultimate result. God knew in eternity past of man's inability to overcome sin and its consequences. In love, He sent His Son, Jesus Christ, who died on a cross to conquer sin and arose from the dead to give us eternal life. When we accept Christ as Lord and Savior, death becomes a temporary separation between us and our loved ones who have accepted Him. The physical body becomes an empty house because the real person living inside has moved out to abide with Jesus in heaven. "We are confident, I say, and willing rather to be absent from the body, and to be present with the Lord" (2 Corinthians 5:8, KJV).

I realized that when Jeffrey died he was transported into the presence of Jesus Christ, my Lord and Savior. Thinking of how much God loved me in providing an eternal home especially for Jeffrey left no room for bitterness in my heart. I could no longer have physical contact with my son, but I could look forward to fellowship forever when someday I join him in Eternity. In spite of this assurance, I grieved over my loss. I began to wonder . . . did Jesus understand my broken heart?

Heartaches and suffering are common to all. While on earth Jesus Christ understood suffering. He experienced grief, fatigue, painful torture, mental abuse, and abandonment. The scope of His life encompassed every trial known to man. In all these things, He did not become bitter. Because of these things, however, we know he identifies with us. He is filled with compassion. He knows and cares when we hurt.

Just as Jesus suffered the cross prior to the Resurrection, often we must go through trials before gaining victory and new insights for living. Jesus obeyed God and did not give up when He was in agony. Likewise, when we are obedient to God during trials and testings, He brings us through triumphantly.

One man in Scripture whose reaction encouraged me was Job. In a blow-by-blow account, I read how Job lost everything—his wealth, his ten children, and eventually his health. He was left with his wife, who told him to "curse God and die" (Job 2:9), and three friends, who tried to convince him that he had done something to deserve God's wrath. They gave him no encouragement. He stood alone.

Humanly speaking, Job did not deserve the catastrophes that befell him. Yet, in all of this, Job humbled himself and acknowledged God as his Creator, the One who gave him everything in the first place. Job recognized the sovereignty of God and His right to bestow blessings or to allow difficulty. Job asked his wife, "Shall we indeed accept good from God and not accept adversity?" (Job 2:10).

Job made a choice about his relationship with God before calamity came. He decided to worship God. This attitude gave Job a teachable spirit. After hearing of the disasters that had befallen him, "Job arose and tore his robe and shaved his head, and he fell to the ground and worshiped. And he said, 'Naked I came from my mother's womb, and naked I shall return there. The LORD gave and the LORD has taken away. Blessed be the name of the LORD'" (Job 1:20-21).

Job suffered grief because of his loss and endured the faulty counsel of others. He was emotionally drained and became depressed. He questioned God's wisdom. However, after all of Job's questioning and searching for answers, God replied, and Job listened. During his trial Job learned patience, and afterward, he knew God more intimately than before.

Dr. Roy B. Zuck writes the following conclusions in his book *Job.* "Job learned that effrontery (i.e. boldness, audacity) in accusing God of injustice was sin—and we, too, should learn the error of challenging God's will and wisdom. A high view of the greatness of God should deepen our sense of humility and awe before Him, removing from us pride and self-sufficiency."

Dr. Zuck continues, "Job was not able to fathom God's mysteries, yet he came to trust the all-perfect God more fully, to realize that God is equally as loving when He sends afflictions as when He sends prosperity."

In conclusion, Dr. Zuck states, "Instead of searching frantically for an elusive answer to the perennial why, the Christian can enjoy life by resting in God. Instead of pounding the walls in angered frustration, he can quietly accept God's designs, knowing that His grace is sufficient (2 Corinthians 12:9), that His way is perfect (Psalm 18:30) and that, as Job learned, He is 'full of compassion and is merciful' (James 5:11)."[13]

God provides for every need I now have or will ever have. I must behold Him—His love, mercy, long-suffering, grace, forgiveness, and sovereignty. After dwelling upon the character of God, I can only marvel that He gives me even one day of life.

Finally, in answer to the question why, I have decided that my reaction to suffering is more important than the cause. I know that because I am a part of a fallen world, I will experience trials and testings. If I never experienced their pressure, I would not cry out to God. I would miss the lessons He desires to teach me. So the question is not, Will I suffer? It is, How will I respond to suffering?

From Hannah Hurnard's *Hind's Feet on High Places* I read this quotation: "As Christians we know, in theory at least, that in the life of a child of God there are no 'second causes,' that even the most unjust and cruel things, as well as all seemingly pointless and undeserved sufferings, have been permitted by God as a glorious opportunity for us to *react* to them in such a way that our Lord and Savior is able to produce in us, little by little, His own lovely character."[14]

Happiness Is a Choice is a book title that intrigues me.[15] I think a parallel statement could also be made that bitterness is a choice, an alternative that hinders spiritual growth.

I once heard singer JoAnn Shelton say, prior to a concert, "Praise moves me from Complaint Avenue to Thanksgiving Boulevard." I have discovered that when my heart is filled with worship and praise to God, there is no room for bitterness.

When submerged in heartache, I must remind myself to lift my eyes above the circumstances and to ask these questions: What does God want to teach me? Am I willing to be conformed to the image of Christ? Will I choose to be bitter or better?

FIFTEEN
How Can God Use This Experience for Good?

For you will have the LORD for an everlasting light, and the days of your mourning will be finished.
Isaiah 60:20

❈ In her book *Affliction* Edith Schaeffer wrote,

Our assurance as children of the Living God is that He is able to bring beauty from ashes and to give the 'oil of joy' for the spirit of mourning (see Isaiah 61:3, KJV). And, in addition, He refines, purifies, proves, and causes to grow in us something precious and lasting in our attitudes toward Him and in our actions to other human beings. As we turn to Him in our affliction and ask for help, He does not allow our affliction to be "wasted."[16]

From my heart I can say that a little boy led me to some great discoveries. God makes no mistakes. He graciously accomplished much in my life through Jeffrey's death that could never have taken place otherwise. Questions were raised that I might never have asked. Answers were found that I might never have sought.

Death was like an urgent message shouted through a megaphone, "Life is short. Life is uncertain. Don't forget to say, 'I love you!'" After Jeffrey left, I looked at my family with new eyes. We have so little time to love and to show love. Each day must count. Ideally, each day must be a complete unit; the sun must not set upon ill will or hurt feelings. We do not have the promise of tomorrow to make it right. Maintaining a valuable relationship is often more important than the issue at hand. We need to evaluate situations carefully and seek to respond in a Christlike manner.

I thought about the privilege of parenting. We only have one opportunity to teach our children, and it comes one day at a time. I have become more aware that the time, effort, and energy we pour into our children's lives is a worthwhile investment. My advice is, Do not put off what you would like to do with your children! Do it now. Love them now. Take time for making special memories. Nuture children with spiritual food. The spiritual dimension does not grow automatically as a child grows physically. It requires active guidance, prayer, and discipline. Children need someone who cares and encourages, someone close when there is a hurt or need.

After Jeffrey's death, I felt the urgency of spiritual training for our children who remained. I realized that I will not always be with them, but if I pass along God's truth to them, and they know Him, they will be sustained through the trials of their own lives just as I've been sustained through mine.

God has helped me to develop a grateful spirit. Each day of life is a gift. Jeffrey's life was a gift, and I'm so thankful for the time we had with him. Even though it was brief, it was wonderful. Jeffrey is not with us here, but he is still part of our family. When I'm asked about our children, I often say, "We have two on earth and one in heaven." I've found reminiscing to be a therapeutic tool in relieving the tension and frustration of his sudden departure. I recall many happy days. Jeffrey was special and will never be forgotten; he could never be replaced.

When Jim and I were at the hospital during Jeffrey's illness, Jim prayed that God would use this experience for our good and for His glory. At that time, we had no idea how this prayer would be answered. One exciting way was through the Sias family.

Earlier I mentioned that while Jim and I were still at Children's Medical Center in Dallas we met a Latin-American woman, Tony Sias, sitting alone in the Intensive Care Unit waiting room. We had conversed briefly. I knew that her infant son, Jesse, was near death due to a congenital heart defect. She and her husband had two preschool girls, and they wanted their baby boy to live.

Mrs. Sias watched quietly for two days as our friends came to pray with us. My friend Johanna had given her a Spanish New Testament, which she began to read. Within minutes of Jeffrey's death, she approached me and asked if we could talk.

In response to her request for privacy, we found a vacant room nearby and I closed the door. In slowly spoken, hesitant English, Mrs. Sias tearfully shared these words: "I see that you give your baby to the Lord. . . . I want you to know that today, I give my baby to the Lord, too. He will never be well. He is so sick. I been watching you. I know God take care of you. I know your baby is with the Lord. He will be OK."

Hearing her words, I was overcome with a flood of conflicting emotions. This little stranger and I wept together. I encouraged her as best I could. I prayed for her son, and that God would give her grace during the waiting period.

About two weeks after Jeffrey's memorial service, Mrs. Sias called from Dallas to tell us that Jesse had died, too. Johanna and I rode to Dallas, attended the memorial service, and took some clothes and toys for her girls. It was a meaningful experience.

Several months passed. I received a letter from Mrs. Sias telling us that she had accepted Christ as her personal Savior and had become affiliated with a local church. In a few years, each daughter was saved. Mrs. Sias says that her husband, who does not speak English, has become a different man, although she cannot express what has happened.

The Sias family has faced many hardships. They have moved many times and suffered through sicknesses, family problems, the death of parents, and other difficulties. Through it all, Mrs. Sias has matured as a Christian. She has taught a Spanish-speaking ladies Bible class in recent years. Her faith in God continues to grow.

While I would not have chosen this particular set of circumstances for witnessing, sharing our faith was a natural event. We planted seeds in a heart that God had already prepared. As a result, new children were born into God's family. The Lord continued to use the experience of Jeffrey's illness for good.

God also used Jeffrey's illness to strengthen our marriage. Unfortunately, I've read of many marriages ending in divorce following the death of a child. Two of the reasons given were blaming the marriage partner for the death and ignoring the needs of the partner during the immediate grief period. Jim and I remained committed to each other and to our marriage. As we looked to the Lord for help, He welded us closer together. Sharing the innermost painful moments helped us develop new sensitivities to one another. The struggle benefited our marriage and further sealed the bond of love.

Although grief was often lonely, we were never alone. Provision had already been made for every need. God had prepared a loving and generous church family and special friends to complement the ministry of our immediate family. I discovered that compassion is sometimes best experienced by silence and a willingness to listen. Beyond anything that was said, I remember the physical presence of others. Several dear friends were always available to listen as I expressed my sorrow. In reflecting upon those painful days, I'm unable to recall their words. However, they gave what I needed most . . . their availability, time, undivided attention, hugs, and tears. They eased my burden of grief by sharing it.

Many wonderful books have been written to enlighten and inspire us, but God's Word is the greatest word of comfort. God is the great Comforter, and His Word is powerful to change us and to lift our spirits. His Holy Spirit applies soothing ointment to our wounded hearts as no one else can do. I was reminded of this as I read these verses in Psalm 119, "My soul cleaves to the dust; revive me according to Thy word" (v. 25). "My soul weeps because of grief; strengthen me according to Thy word" (v. 28). "This is my comfort in my affliction, that Thy word has revived me" (v. 50). His Word and His love lifted me from the darkness of grief.

Also, there is power in praise. Sometimes Angie crawls into her daddy's lap and with a big hug and beaming smile states, "Daddy, I love you." This indicates that she willingly and gratefully acknowledges him as her father, knowing that he cares for her and will protect her. Her voluntary expression of love greatly pleases her dad. After Jeffrey's death, I could not understand the reasons why. I found no easy answers, but I did reaffirm my trust in God. The praise I learned to offer was an attitude of quiet, firm, confident assurance in a great and mighty God. As Angie's voluntary expression of love makes her daddy very happy, I, too, can express praise to my heavenly Father and bring Him joy.

Further, I discovered the difference between happiness and joy. Happiness may depend upon temporal or material things. It may even thrive as a response to other people. However, if things or people are taken away, what is left? There is a void inside us meant for God alone. No person or thing will fill it, only God Himself. When He is present in our lives, we are aware of peace that cannot be humanly explained. Regardless of changing circumstances or the removal of temporal things, we experience joy.

For the first time, I understood how suffering prepares us for Christ's coming. "Beloved, do not be surprised at the fiery ordeal among you, which comes upon you for your testing, as though some strange thing were happening to you; but to the degree that you share the sufferings of Christ, keep on rejoicing; so that also at the revelation of His glory, you may rejoice with exultation" (1 Peter 4:12-13).

As believers, we experience times of ecstasy as well as times of great sorrow. We are not to lose sight of our purpose in life; we are not to become so caught up in the pleasures of this world that we forget we belong to Christ. We were bought with a price. If we never suffered, we would become complacent and contented here on earth. After a time of suffering, we begin to look hopefully to the day when all suffering will cease. We look forward to Christ's coming with great anticipation. We will rejoice!

And finally, I learned that it is one thing to grieve without understanding, but quite another to grieve with hope. Jesus Christ is the giver of life, and when He indwells us, life no longer becomes a downhill slide toward death but rather an exciting upward trek toward God. Our grief in the loss of a loved one is painful; it is agonizing. However, Jesus said, "If anyone keeps My word, he shall never see death" (John 8:51). Our hope is the assurance that while our bodies will eventually wear out, spiritual death will never happen. We will never be separated from the presence and love of God.

While all of us are part of the human family, only those who have invited Jesus Christ into their lives are part of God's family. Author David Hubbard writes, "For those who belong to Him, death may hold twinges of anxiety, but the ultimate terror is gone."[17]

One day while reflecting upon the rich lessons I'd learned since Jeffrey's departure, I remembered a note I'd written soon after he left us. When I found it and read it over again, the words still brought comfort and hope. In closing, I'd like to share them with you.

Dear Jeffrey,

There was something very special about you from the beginning. I could not explain it. Perhaps it was the twinkle in your bright blue eyes or your zest for life. You were with us for such a short time, but Daddy and I loved you very much. We enjoyed every minute. Steve and Angie loved you, too. We all miss you and wish you were with us, but the Good Shepherd gathered you into His gentle arms and took you to a better place. As I walk with the Lord each day, I know I am close to you. We'll see you later, Jeffrey. Then, we'll be together forever.

I love you dearly,
Mom

NOTES

[1] Joanne Marxhausen, *If I Should Die, If I Should Live* (St. Louis, Mo.: Concordia Publishing House, 1975).

[2] J. Vernon McGee, *Death of a Little Child* (Pasadena, Calif.: Thru the Bible Radio, 1970).

[3] Joyce Landorf, *Mourning Song* (Old Tappan, N.J.: Fleming H. Revell Company, 1974).

[4] Gary R. Collins, *Overcoming Anxiety* (Santa Ana, Calif.: Vision House Publishers, 1973).

[5] Jay E. Adams, *The Christian Counselor's Manual* (Grand Rapids, Mich.: Baker Book House, 1973), 414-415.

[6] Ibid.

[7] J. R. Miller, *Words of Comfort* (Chattanooga, Tenn.: AMG Publishers, n.d.), 96-97.

[8] R. C. Sproul, *Effective Prayer* (Carol Stream, Ill.: Tyndale House Publishers, 1984), 71-72.

[9]Deuteronomy 3:23-25 (Moses), 1 Kings 29:4 (Elijah), 2 Corinthians 12:8-9 (Paul).

[10]Samuel Chadwick, *God Listens to the Crying Heart in the Secret Place* (Westchester, Ill.: Good News Publishers, 1973), 83-88.

[11]Rosalind Rinker, *Prayer, Conversing with God* (Grand Rapids, Mich.: Zondervan Publishing House, 1959).

[12]Corrie ten Boom, *The Hiding Place* (Old Tappan, N.J.: Fleming H. Revell Co., 1971), 29.

[13]Roy B. Zuck, *Job* (Chicago, Ill.: Moody Press, 1978), 190-191.

[14]Hannah Hurnard, *Hind's Feet on High Places* (Carol Stream, Ill.: Tyndale House Publishers, Inc., 1977), 10-11.

[15]Frank B. Minirth, M.D., and Paul D. Meier, M.D., *Happiness Is a Choice* (Grand Rapids, Mich.: Baker Book House, 1978).

[16]Edith Schaeffer, *Affliction* (Old Tappan, N.J.: Fleming H. Revell Company, 1978), 160.

[17]David H. Hubbard, *How to Face Your Fears* (New York: A. J. Holman Company, 1972), 129.